THE TRIPLE EEE TRACK

Secret Formula for Lasting Success

Dr Mukesh Aggarwal

CONTENTS

PREFACE

Success is a journey, not a destination. Yet, in a world where change is constant and challenges abound, how do we ensure our success endures? This question has intrigued humanity for centuries. As I delved into the patterns of high achievers across various fields, I realized there is no singular path to success—there are, instead, guiding principles. And from these, I crafted a framework: the Triple EEE Track.

The Triple EEE Track—Execute, Evaluate, and Evolve—is a simple yet profound formula designed to transform your approach to personal and professional success. It isn't about one-time victories or fleeting moments of triumph; rather, it is a mindset that promotes lasting growth and fulfillment. The EEE Track is the key to thriving in an unpredictable world, where the ability to take action, learn from experience, and adapt to change is more valuable than any shortcut or secret formula.

In Part I of this book, we explore the art of Execution—the essential power of taking action. Dreams and goals only materialize when we move beyond planning and into doing. This section lays the foundation, showing you how to overcome inertia and turn intention into tangible results.

In Part II, we delve into Evaluation. Success is not just about moving forward; it's about moving in the right direction. Here, I reveal the importance of reflection—how to pause, analyze, and learn from your efforts, ensuring that every action refines your approach.

Finally, in Part III, we look at how to Evolve. The world is always changing, and so must we. Through growth and adaptation, we transform into better versions of ourselves. This section will guide you through the process of self-renewal, making sure that your success is not just temporary but sustained over the long term.

Throughout the book, you will find case studies, tools, and techniques that bring the EEE Track to life, along with practical applications that allow you to integrate it into your daily routine. You will also encounter the science behind long-term success and the challenges you may face on this journey.

Success is not just for the lucky or the talented—it is for those who are willing to follow a disciplined process. The Triple EEE Track is your roadmap to achieving not only your immediate goals but also a life of meaningful, lasting success.

Let us embark on this journey together.

— Dr. Mukesh Aggarwal

Chapter 1

INTRODUCTION
THE EEE TRACK

Success, in any sphere of life, is rarely the result of a single stroke of brilliance. More often, it emerges from a process of continuous action, reflection, and adaptation. This is the foundation of the Triple EEE Track—Execute, Evaluate, and Evolve—a powerful framework designed to guide you through a lifelong journey of sustained achievement and growth.

In this chapter, we'll explore the essence of the EEE cycle, how it mirrors the process of biological evolution, and how it aligns with the science of habit formation. By understanding the cycle of action, feedback, and growth, you'll be equipped to use the EEE Track as a compass for navigating both challenges and opportunities in your personal and professional life.

Defining EEE: The Cycle of Action, Feedback, and Growth

At its core, the Triple EEE Track represents a continuous loop of Execution, Evaluation, and Evolution:

Execute: The act of taking deliberate, meaningful action. This is where intention meets reality. Without execution, even the best ideas remain unfulfilled potential.

Evaluate: Once an action is taken, it must be followed by thoughtful reflection. This stage is about analyzing outcomes, gathering feedback, and asking critical **questions:** What worked? What didn't? What can be improved?

Evolve: Armed with the insights from evaluation, you are ready to adapt. This is where growth happens, where you refine your approach and evolve into a more capable version of yourself. Whether the goal is to improve a skill, achieve a career milestone, or enhance personal well-being, evolution is the key to making sure progress is ongoing.

This cycle is not a one-time process but a continuous one. Each phase feeds into the next, creating a dynamic system of constant learning and improvement. By committing to the EEE cycle, you embrace a path that transforms your goals from mere aspirations into lasting achievements.

Evolution of the Concept: From Darwinism to Personal Transformation

The concept of the EEE Track is rooted in the principles of adaptation and survival that have long been part of our natural world. Charles Darwin's theory of evolution, which emphasizes "survival of the fittest," offers a compelling metaphor for how individuals and organizations succeed over time.

In biological evolution, species that adapt to their environments thrive, while those that fail to evolve often perish. Similarly, in the realm of personal growth, those who continuously adapt and improve their strategies are more likely to succeed. The EEE Track operates on this same principle of evolution, only instead of biological traits, it focuses on our actions, decisions, and mindset.

Think of your personal and professional life as an ecosystem. Just as species must execute actions to survive (finding food, protecting themselves, reproducing), you must execute tasks to achieve success. Similarly, biological adaptation requires feedback—animals learn from their environment to avoid danger or improve their chances of survival. In the same way, we must evaluate the feedback we receive from our efforts, reflecting on what helps us thrive and what holds us back. Finally, evolution in nature takes time, just as our personal evolution takes place over repeated cycles of growth and learning.

The EEE Track is, in essence, a roadmap for navigating this ongoing transformation. Just as organisms evolve through natural selection, we evolve by learning from our experiences and adapting our strategies for future success.

The Science of Habits: How EEE Fits into the Habit Loop

Success, as we know, is often the product of habits—those automatic behaviors that shape our daily lives. Charles Duhigg, in his book The Power of Habit, explains how habits form through a process known as the "habit loop," which consists of three key components:

1. Cue: A trigger that initiates the behavior.
2. Routine: The behavior itself, performed in response to the cue.

3. Reward: The positive reinforcement that encourages the behavior to continue.

The habit loop is a cycle, much like the EEE Track, and the two frameworks align in powerful ways. When we execute an action (routine), we do so in response to some kind of cue—perhaps a desire to achieve a goal, solve a problem, or improve a situation. After execution, we enter the evaluation stage, where we reflect on the outcome (reward or lack thereof). This reflection becomes feedback, which informs how we evolve, refining the action or behavior for future success.

Let's break it down:

Cue (Execution): The trigger for taking action. Whether it's a desire for success, a pressing need, or a specific goal, execution begins with a cue.

Routine (Evaluation): The act of reflection. After every action, we analyze the outcomes, just as we analyze the routine in the habit loop.

Reward (Evolution): The final result, whether positive or negative, informs how we evolve. If the reward is positive, we reinforce the behavior. If it's negative, we adjust our approach.

By applying the EEE Track within the habit loop, we can create a system for continuous improvement. Each time we execute a task, we are reinforcing a behavior that, with evaluation, helps us evolve. Over time, this cycle not only fosters growth but also solidifies success as a habit itself.

EEE: A Path to Lasting Success

The brilliance of the Triple EEE Track lies in its simplicity. It is not a complicated formula, nor does it require vast resources or talent. Instead, it relies on a disciplined approach to action, reflection, and adaptation. Whether you are an entrepreneur seeking to grow your business, a student striving for academic excellence, or someone looking to improve their health or relationships, the EEE Track can guide you toward your goals.

By adopting this framework, you will develop resilience in the face of setbacks and learn how to convert challenges into opportunities for growth. The EEE Track ensures that you are not just repeating the same actions, but that each cycle brings you closer to lasting success.

In the chapters that follow, we will explore each stage of the EEE Track in greater detail, with practical strategies and real-world examples that demonstrate its effectiveness. You will discover how to harness the power of execution, master the art of evaluation, and embrace evolution as a lifelong journey. Together, these elements form the secret formula for success that endures.

Let's begin this journey of transformation and lasting achievement with the Triple EEE Track.

Chapter 2

PART I

EXECUTE: THE POWER OF TAKING ACTION

Success is built on action. No matter how brilliant an idea, how well-thought-out a plan, or how high the motivation, nothing happens until action is taken. Execution is the bridge between potential and achievement. Yet, for many, this is where the journey gets stuck. We get lost in planning, paralyzed by over-analysis, or overwhelmed by the enormity of the task ahead.

In this chapter, we will dive into the neuroscience of action, explore how our brains are wired for movement, and discuss why taking the first step is often the most crucial. We'll also confront the common challenge of "paralysis by analysis" and learn how to overcome it. Finally, we'll look at the power of micro-execution and how starting small can lead to massive results over time.

The Neuroscience of Action: How the Brain Prepares for Movement

Action begins in the brain, specifically in the prefrontal cortex, which is responsible for decision-making and planning. This part of the brain is like the control center that decides when, where, and how we take action. However, before any action occurs, the brain must prepare for it.

Research shows that as soon as you decide to perform an action, your brain starts sending signals to various parts of the body, preparing you to execute that decision. This process begins long before you consciously realize it. The brain essentially "warms up" for the task by creating a mental simulation of the action. Once the action is performed, the brain rewards you with a surge of dopamine—a neurotransmitter associated with pleasure and motivation.

This dopamine release is crucial because it reinforces behavior. It's the brain's way of telling you, "Well done, keep going." The more you execute, the more dopamine your brain releases, creating a cycle of motivation and action. This is why the first step is so important—it sets off a chain reaction that keeps you moving forward.

This neurological reward system explains why action, no matter how small, is essential to momentum. Once you start, the brain rewards you, making it easier to continue. The power of execution lies in this feedback loop between action and reward, where each step forward fuels the next.

Overcoming Paralysis by Analysis: The Decision-Making Trap

While action is rewarding, many of us struggle to take that first step. We get trapped in endless cycles of planning, researching, and analyzing our options. This phenomenon, known as "paralysis by analysis," is common when we overthink decisions and hesitate to act.
In his book Thinking, Fast and Slow, psychologist Daniel Kahneman explores how humans make decisions. He explains that our brains operate using two systems: System 1, which is fast, instinctive, and emotional, and System 2, which is slower, more deliberate, and analytical. While both

systems have their advantages, over-reliance on System 2—where we analyze every possible outcome—can lead to indecision.

Kahneman's research shows that we often fall into the trap of wanting to make the "perfect" decision, weighing all the pros and cons until we are immobilized by complexity. This desire for perfection can hinder execution because the more we overthink; the harder it becomes to act.

To break free from paralysis by analysis, it's essential to shift from overthinking to action. One effective way is to set a decision-making deadline. By limiting the time spent analyzing, you force yourself to make a choice and move forward. Another strategy is to embrace the concept of "good enough" decisions, recognizing that perfection is often the enemy of progress. By accepting that your first steps don't have to be flawless, you free yourself to take action and refine your approach along the way.

Micro-Execution: The Power of Starting Small

In Atomic Habits, James Clear introduces the concept of micro-execution—the idea that small, consistent actions can lead to significant results over time. This is especially important when tackling large goals, which can often feel overwhelming.

Clear argues that the key to overcoming this overwhelm is to break down large tasks into the smallest possible steps. By focusing on micro-execution, you build momentum, create positive habits, and accumulate incremental progress. Each small action might seem insignificant on its own, but compounded over time, these small actions lead to transformative outcomes.

Consider the difference between setting a vague goal, like "I want to get fit," versus starting with a micro-execution strategy: "I will do five minutes of exercise every day." The latter is concrete, manageable, and easy to execute. As you consistently take these small steps, the habit strengthens, and the effort required maintaining it decreases. Eventually, five minutes of exercise becomes 10, then 20, and soon you've built a sustainable fitness routine.

This concept applies to all areas of life, from career goals to personal development. The secret is to start small and let consistency compound over time. Each small action contributes to a larger result, much like how drops of water eventually fill a bucket. Micro-execution transforms daunting goals into achievable steps, removing the mental barriers to taking action.

Action Breeds Confidence

One of the most remarkable effects of taking action is the confidence it builds. Often, we mistakenly believe that we need confidence before we can take action. In reality, confidence is the result of action, not the precursor. Each time you execute, you reinforce your ability to achieve, and that success fuels further confidence.

By consistently executing, even on a small scale, you develop a sense of mastery over time. This growing confidence not only helps you take bigger steps in the future but also reduces the anxiety associated with decision-making and execution. In short, action builds momentum, and momentum builds confidence.

The Ripple Effect of Execution

Action has a ripple effect. Once you begin executing on a small scale, that execution influences other areas of your life. The discipline you build in one domain, such as sticking to a morning routine or completing daily tasks, often spills over into other domains, such as work, relationships, or personal goals.

This ripple effect is powerful because success in one area often leads to improvements in others. As you build positive habits and take consistent action, you start to see the benefits accumulate in ways you may not have initially anticipated. This is the essence of micro-execution—small, consistent steps that lead to major changes over time.

Conclusion: The Power Lies in Doing

The first step is always the hardest, but it is also the most important. Execution is the catalyst that turns your ideas, plans, and dreams into reality. Whether you're looking to build a new skill, achieve a professional goal, or make a personal transformation, it all begins with action.

Remember, the brain is wired to reward action. The simple act of starting triggers a dopamine response, reinforcing your motivation and making it easier to continue. Don't let overthinking or fear of imperfection hold you back. Start small, execute consistently, and watch as those small actions compound into lasting success.

In the next chapter, we will explore the second stage of the EEE Track: Evaluate. Once action has been taken, how do we reflect on and learn from our efforts? How can we ensure that each action brings us closer to our ultimate goals? Join me as we dive into the art of thoughtful evaluation.

Chapter 3

PART II
EVALUATE: LEARNING THROUGH REFLECTION

Execution is only the beginning. After taking action, the next critical step is to pause and evaluate. Without reflection, we cannot learn from our successes or failures, and without learning, we cannot improve. Evaluation is where growth happens. It is the feedback loop that allows us to course-correct, refine our actions, and move closer to our goals.

In this chapter, we will explore the concept of feedback loops, both in nature and human behavior. We'll look at how self-assessment plays a critical role in personal development and how adopting a growth mindset can unlock our potential. We'll also examine the role of biases in evaluation and how to conduct assessments in a way that minimizes these biases, leading to more accurate and productive reflections.

Feedback Loops in Nature: The Role of Evaluation in Balance

Evaluation is a process embedded in the natural world. In biology, feedback loops are critical to maintaining balance, a process known as homeostasis. Our bodies are constantly evaluating internal conditions—like temperature, pH, and glucose levels—against a set of optimal values. When something goes out of range, the body responds with adjustments to bring it back into balance.

For example, when your body temperature rises, sweat glands activate to cool you down. When your blood sugar drops, your body releases stored energy to keep you going. These feedback loops are continuous cycles of monitoring, adjusting, and recalibrating, ensuring that the system remains balanced.

The same principle applies to our personal and professional lives. After every action, we need to evaluate its results and make adjustments based on what we learn. This process of continuous feedback and adjustment keeps us aligned with our goals. Just as the body maintains balance through homeostasis, we can maintain progress through reflection and evaluation.

The Power of Self-Assessment: Unlocking Growth through Reflection

Self-assessment is a powerful tool for growth. When we take the time to honestly evaluate our actions, we gain valuable insights into what worked, what didn't, and why. This process of reflection fosters learning and sets the stage for improvement.

One of the most influential voices on the topic of self-assessment is Carol Dweck, a psychologist known for her work on the growth mindset. In her research, Dweck found that people with a growth mindset—those who believe that their abilities and intelligence can be developed—are more likely to embrace challenges, persist through difficulties, and ultimately achieve more than those with a fixed mindset, who believe their abilities are static.

For people with a growth mindset, evaluation is not just about measuring success; it's about learning from both successes and failures. They see failure as an opportunity to grow rather than as a reflection of their limitations. By evaluating their performance and identifying areas for improvement, they foster continuous growth.

Incorporating Dweck's growth mindset into your evaluation process is transformative. Instead of fearing failure or criticism, embrace evaluation as a learning tool. Every setback becomes an opportunity for growth. The key is to approach self-assessment with honesty, curiosity, and a willingness to learn. When you evaluate your actions with this mindset, you become better equipped to make meaningful progress in all areas of life.

Bias in Evaluation: Avoiding Cognitive Traps

While evaluation is essential for growth, it's not always straightforward. Our brains are wired with cognitive biases that can distort our evaluations, leading us to incorrect conclusions. To conduct effective evaluations, we must be aware of these biases and take steps to minimize their impact.

One common bias is confirmation bias, the tendency to seek out or interpret information in a way that confirms our preexisting beliefs. For example, if you believe that you are not good at public speaking, you may focus on the few mistakes you made during a presentation rather than the moments when you communicated effectively. This selective focus reinforces your negative self-perception and prevents you from seeing the full picture.

Another bias is hindsight bias, where we view past events as more predictable than they actually were. After a failure, hindsight bias might lead you to think, "I should have seen that coming," even if the outcome was genuinely unpredictable. This can lead to unnecessary self-blame or, conversely, an overconfidence that blinds you to potential risks in the future.

To minimize these biases, it's important to adopt a structured approach to evaluation. Here are some strategies:

Seek objective data: Look for measurable outcomes rather than relying on subjective feelings. For example, instead of thinking, "I feel like that meeting didn't go well," ask, "What were the specific outcomes? Did I achieve the goals I set?"

Get external feedback: Ask others for their perspective. Often, we are too close to our own actions to evaluate them accurately. Trusted colleagues, friends, or mentors can provide valuable insights that we might miss.

Record your thoughts and results: Keeping a journal of your actions and reflections can help you see patterns over time. Writing down what you learned from each experience forces you to engage in a deeper level of reflection and helps you spot biases that may be clouding your judgment.

Challenge your assumptions: Before drawing conclusions, ask yourself, "Is this belief based on evidence, or is it a product of my biases?" Actively questioning your assumptions helps counteract the influence of cognitive biases.

By being mindful of these biases and actively working to counter them, you can conduct more accurate evaluations and gain deeper insights into your performance. This, in turn, leads to more effective adjustments and, ultimately, better results.

The Role of Emotion in Evaluation

Another factor that can influence evaluation is emotion. When we're too emotionally invested in a particular outcome, our ability to evaluate it objectively is compromised. For example, if you've worked incredibly hard on a project, you might be overly critical if it doesn't turn out exactly as you envisioned, or you might overlook flaws because you're too attached to the effort you put in.

Emotional detachment doesn't mean ignoring your feelings; it means learning to separate your emotional response from the actual results. A good strategy is to give yourself time and space before evaluating something you feel strongly about. Stepping away for a day or two can help you gain perspective, allowing for a more balanced and fair assessment.

The Benefits of Consistent Evaluation

Consistent evaluation, like consistent execution, is key to long-term success. The more often you evaluate your actions, the more opportunities you have to adjust and improve. This is where the cycle of the EEE Track—Execute, Evaluate, Evolve—comes into play. After each execution, you evaluate. After each evaluation, you evolve your approach. This constant cycle of action and reflection ensures that you are always learning, growing, and improving.

Evaluation helps you avoid repeating mistakes and identifies areas where small changes can make a big difference. It also keeps you accountable, ensuring that you remain aligned with your goals. When you make evaluation a regular part of your routine, you create a powerful feedback loop that drives continuous improvement.

Conclusion: Reflection as a Path to Mastery

Evaluation is not about judgment; it's about learning. It's the process that turns action into growth and ensures that each step forward is informed by the lessons of the past. Whether you're reflecting on a small daily habit or a major life decision, the practice of evaluation allows you to refine your approach and move closer to mastery.

In the next chapter, we'll explore the third part of the EEE Track: Evolve. How do we adapt and grow from the insights gained through evaluation? How can we transform reflection into action and ensure that our growth is continuous and sustainable? Join me as we delve into the process of evolution, both personal and professional.

Chapter 4

PART III

EVOLVE: ADAPTATION THROUGH GROWTH

In the journey to lasting success, adaptation is one of the most powerful forces driving human potential. Like all living organisms, humans must continuously evolve, not just physically but mentally and emotionally. This chapter delves into the science of neuroplasticity, evolutionary psychology, and resilience, illustrating how these forces combine to shape our ability to grow, adapt, and ultimately, succeed.

Neuroplasticity: The Brain's Capacity for Change

One of the most fascinating aspects of human evolution is the brain's ability to change and adapt over time, a phenomenon known as neuroplasticity. Neuroplasticity refers to the brain's capacity to reorganize itself by forming new neural connections throughout life. This ability allows the brain to adjust to new learning experiences, environments, and challenges.

Studies on neuroplasticity have revealed that learning a new skill or acquiring knowledge physically reshapes the brain's structure. For instance, research involving London taxi drivers found that their hippocampus, the part of the brain responsible for spatial memory, was significantly larger than that of the average person. This growth was attributed to the rigorous memorization of the city's intricate streets. Another study on bilingual individuals found that learning a second language increased gray matter density in areas of the brain related to language acquisition.

The key takeaway from these studies is that learning and adapting are lifelong processes. The more we engage in deliberate practice, the more our brain rewires itself to optimize performance. This concept is crucial for success in any endeavor. Whether it's learning a new skill, overcoming a setback, or expanding one's capabilities, neuroplasticity shows that our brains are not fixed; they are dynamic, evolving with every experience.

Evolutionary Psychology: Evolving in Response to Feedback

The concept of "survival of the fittest," as described by Charles Darwin, offers valuable insights into human behavior and growth. While Darwin's theory originally focused on physical evolution, the underlying principles of adaptation and feedback apply equally to personal development. Evolutionary psychology suggests that human behaviors and thought patterns have evolved over time in response to environmental pressures, leading to the development of survival strategies that have shaped who we are today.

In a modern context, evolution doesn't merely mean physical survival but also thriving through cognitive and emotional adaptation. Feedback plays a crucial role in this evolutionary process. Just as early humans evolved in response to environmental challenges, individuals today must adapt to the feedback they receive in their personal and professional lives. Whether it's criticism from a mentor, market data for a business, or feedback from colleagues, the ability to evolve depends on how well we integrate these external inputs into our growth trajectory.

The difference between those who stagnate and those who thrive lies in their capacity to respond to feedback with action. Evolutionary success is no longer about physical dominance, but about mental agility, emotional resilience, and the ability to evolve one's strategy in response to ever-changing circumstances.

Resilience through Evolution: Grit and the Power of Persistence

Resilience is another critical component of adaptation and growth, and no one has captured this better than psychologist Angela Duckworth in her work on grit. Grit, defined as a combination of passion and perseverance, is often the determining factor in whether a person can evolve beyond failure and reach their long-term goals.

Duckworth's research demonstrates that talent alone is not enough for success. Instead, the ability to persist through challenges, learn from failures, and continue evolving toward a goal is what distinguishes high achievers from the rest. She argues that grit is more predictive of success than IQ, talent, or even social intelligence. This persistence, she posits, enables individuals to bounce back from setbacks, grow stronger, and continue on their path to mastery.

Resilience, therefore, is not just the ability to withstand failure but the capacity to use failure as fuel for growth. Each setback offers a unique opportunity for learning and adaptation, much like how organisms evolve in response to environmental changes. Those who embody grit don't just survive—they thrive, using each challenge as a stepping stone for further growth.

The Triple EEE Formula: Evolve through Constant Growth

The final phase of the Triple EEE Track—Evolve—emphasizes the need for continuous adaptation and growth. Neuroplasticity proves that we can change our brains at any stage in life, opening the door to limitless learning. Evolutionary psychology shows that adaptation to feedback is key to personal and professional evolution. And grit, as described by Angela Duckworth, is the driving force that allows us to persist, learn, and grow from each challenge.

In this phase, success is not defined by a singular moment of achievement but by an ongoing process of evolving in response to the world around us. To truly evolve, we must embrace change, seek feedback, and cultivate resilience. It's about recognizing that every experience, whether good or bad, is an opportunity for growth. The road to lasting success is not a straight line, but a constantly shifting journey that requires us to evolve at every step.

This is the essence of the Evolve phase—growing not just for the sake of success, but as a way to unlock our full potential and adapt to life's endless changes.

Chapter 5

CASE STUDIES
EEE IN ACTION

The Execute, Evaluate, and Evolve (EEE) framework is not just a theoretical model; it's a proven strategy employed by some of the world's most successful businesses, individuals, and inventors. This chapter delves into real-world examples to illustrate how the EEE process works in practice and how it has driven innovation, personal development, and business success.

1. Business Applications: The Power of Agile Methods and Feedback Loops

Apple: Iteration and Evolution in Product Development

Apple's journey to becoming one of the most innovative companies in the world is deeply rooted in the principles of EEE. Apple's success is not only about brilliant designs but also about continuous execution, evaluation, and evolution.

When Steve Jobs returned to Apple in 1997, the company was struggling, but Jobs applied the EEE model to transform Apple into a market leader. Execution began with a focus on simplicity and cutting-edge technology, embodied in the release of the iMac, a bold product that broke away from conventional computer design. But Apple didn't stop at a single product launch. Each new iteration of their products—whether the iPod, iPhone, or Macbook—was the result of thorough evaluation of user feedback, market trends, and internal reviews.

Apple uses customer feedback extensively to evolve its products. For instance, after the launch of the first iPhone, the company listened to critiques about battery life, screen size, and app functionality. Each new generation addressed these issues while introducing innovative features like the App Store and facial recognition technology. This continuous process of executing, evaluating, and evolving is at the heart of Apple's success, enabling the company to maintain its competitive edge.

Toyota: The Kaizen Approach and Lean Manufacturing

Toyota is another business giant that exemplifies the EEE framework through its Kaizen philosophy, which translates to "continuous improvement." Toyota's production system is one of the best examples of how execution, evaluation, and evolution can drive success, not just for the company, but for an entire industry.

Toyota's Lean Manufacturing system focuses on executing small, manageable changes and then carefully evaluating their effectiveness in reducing waste, increasing efficiency, and improving quality. Employees at all levels are encouraged to suggest improvements, creating a feedback loop that drives innovation and problem-solving from the ground up.

The evaluate phase at Toyota is where data-driven decision-making comes into play. Every change is carefully monitored and evaluated using real-time data on production speed, defects, and customer satisfaction. Once the evaluation phase is complete, the company evolves its production processes, integrating the most effective strategies and discarding inefficient practices.

Toyota's system demonstrates that evolution isn't always about dramatic shifts; it's about small, incremental improvements that compound over time to create massive impact. This method of constant iteration has helped Toyota maintain its position as a leader in the global automotive market for decades.

Here are five Indian case studies that demonstrate the Execute, Evaluate, and Evolve (EEE) framework in action across various sectors, showcasing innovation, personal growth, and business success:

Tata Motors: Transforming Indian Automotive Industry

Tata Motors, part of the Tata Group, applied the EEE framework to transform itself from a domestic player into a global automotive leader. Their development of the Tata Nano is a prime example.

Execution: Tata Motors identified a need for an affordable car for the Indian middle class. They launched the Tata Nano in 2009, marketed as the world's cheapest car.

Evaluation: While the initial launch generated a lot of buzz, sales were underwhelming due to perceptions of low quality and safety concerns. Tata Motors evaluated the reasons for failure, including poor marketing strategies and a lack of focus on consumer aspirations.

Evolution: The company went back to the drawing board and evolved its approach. They improved the product design, focused on quality and safety, and diversified their portfolio to cater to broader segments of the market. This iterative process helped Tata Motors regain its position, especially with other successful models like Tata Tiago and Nexon.

This case shows how Tata Motors continuously evaluated and evolved its strategy to succeed in the competitive automotive industry.

Amul: Building a Dairy Cooperative Movement

Amul, one of India's largest dairy cooperatives, epitomizes the EEE framework through its dynamic adaptation to market and community needs.

Execution: In 1946, under the leadership of Dr. Verghese Kurien, Amul was formed as a cooperative to empower farmers and improve milk production in Gujarat.

Evaluation: Amul consistently evaluated both supply chain operations and market demand. They introduced better practices for milk procurement, developed new products like butter and cheese, and adopted new technology for milk processing.

Evolution: The evolution came in their brand strategy. Amul launched iconic advertising campaigns that became a part of Indian culture, while also diversifying into new markets such as ice cream, chocolates, and paneer. The cooperative evolved its distribution network to become one of the most extensive in India, with modernized production facilities that adhere to global standards.

Amul's growth from a small cooperative to a national dairy giant is a testament to its ability to execute, evaluate, and evolve while maintaining strong community ties.

Zomato: Reinventing Food Delivery in India

Zomato, the Indian food delivery and restaurant discovery platform, is a tech company that used the EEE framework to disrupt the food industry.

Execution: Zomato started in 2008 as a restaurant discovery platform, providing menus and reviews. As they executed this model, they realized the potential for food delivery services.

Evaluation: Through data-driven evaluation, Zomato identified issues like delivery inefficiencies, customer dissatisfaction, and high competition in the food delivery sector. They also recognized that restaurants needed more robust tech solutions to handle orders.

Evolution: Zomato evolved by introducing features like hyperlocal delivery, AI-driven recommendations, and innovative subscription models like Zomato Gold. They also improved their app interface to enhance customer experience and built strong partnerships with restaurants. Their IPO in 2021 marked a new chapter of growth, positioning them as a leader in India's food-tech space.

Zomato's rise demonstrates the importance of adapting to customer needs and refining business models based on continual feedback and evaluation.

Flipkart: Evolving from Books to E-Commerce Giant

Flipkart, India's largest e-commerce platform is a classic example of how the EEE framework can be applied to scale a business from a startup to a market leader.

Execution: Flipkart began as an online bookstore in 2007, with founders Sachin and Binny Bansal executing their vision of delivering books to customers across India.

Evaluation: As the business grew, Flipkart evaluated the needs of the Indian consumer. They found that consumers wanted a broader range of products and a more reliable delivery system. They also assessed customer feedback on delivery times, pricing, and product quality.

Evolution: Based on these evaluations, Flipkart expanded into a full-fledged e-commerce platform offering electronics, fashion, and household products. The company evolved by introducing Cash on Delivery, robust logistics, and the Big Billion Days sale, which revolutionized online shopping in India. Their acquisition by Walmart in 2018 solidified their position as a dominant player in Indian e-commerce.

Flipkart's ability to pivot from books to an expansive e-commerce platform shows how businesses can evolve through constant evaluation of market trends and customer behavior.

2. Personal Growth Stories: Overcoming Obstacles with EEE

Dhirubhai Ambani: The Visionary Who Built Reliance

Dhirubhai Ambani, the founder of Reliance Industries, is an inspiring example of how personal resilience and the Execute, Evaluate, and Evolve (EEE) framework can lead to monumental success.

Execution: Dhirubhai started small, working as a clerk in Yemen before returning to India with a vision to create one of the largest business empires. In 1966, he founded Reliance Commercial Corporation, initially trading in spices and textiles. His strategy was to execute a low-cost, high-volume business model, and he launched the "Vimal" brand, which became synonymous with quality fabrics at affordable prices.

Evaluation: As the business grew, Dhirubhai constantly evaluated market trends, consumer demands, and technological advancements. He understood that in order to expand, Reliance needed to venture into manufacturing. However, rather than sticking solely to textiles, Dhirubhai evaluated the potential of petrochemicals and diversified Reliance's portfolio.

Evolution: Dhirubhai evolved his business from trading textiles to building a petrochemical giant. He also revolutionized fundraising by introducing the idea of equity ownership to ordinary Indians, making Reliance Industries the first company in India to raise significant capital through public investments. His continual adaptation, including vertical integration from textiles to petrochemicals to telecom, turned Reliance into a multi-billion-dollar conglomerate, transforming India's corporate landscape.

Ambani's personal journey demonstrates how continuous evaluation of opportunities and a willingness to evolve led to the creation of one of the largest and most diversified businesses in India.

2. Dr. A.P.J. Abdul Kalam: From Scientist to People's President

Dr. A.P.J. Abdul Kalam, known as the "Missile Man of India," is an iconic figure whose life exemplifies the EEE concept. His journey from a humble background to becoming the President of India is marked by his relentless execution, continuous evaluation, and constant evolution.

Execution: Born into a modest family in Rameswaram, Tamil Nadu, Dr. Kalam pursued aeronautical engineering with a vision to contribute to India's space and defense sectors. He started his career at the Defence Research and Development Organization (DRDO) and later joined the Indian Space Research Organisation (ISRO). His commitment to executing India's space ambitions led to his key role in developing India's first satellite launch vehicle (SLV-III) that successfully deployed the Rohini satellite in 1980.

Evaluation: Throughout his career, Dr. Kalam evaluated India's defense and space capabilities, understanding the need for self-reliance in missile technology. He led the Integrated Guided Missile Development Program (IGMDP), overseeing the development of missiles like Agni and Prith-

vi. His evaluation of India's strategic needs ensured that these projects aligned with the country's long-term security objectives.

Evolution: Dr. Kalam evolved from being a scientist to a statesman. After his illustrious career in science and technology, he transitioned into the role of India's President (2002–2007), where he focused on inspiring youth, promoting education, and advocating for India's development vision, encapsulated in his concept of "Vision 2020." His transformation from a technical leader to the "People's President" demonstrates how he continuously evolved to serve the nation in various capacities.

Dr. Kalam's life story is a perfect example of the EEE framework, showing how perseverance in execution, rigorous self-assessment, and a willingness to adapt and evolve can lead to both personal and national success.

J.K. Rowling: From Rejection to Global Success

Before J.K. Rowling became a household name, she faced a barrage of rejections. Her journey to literary stardom is a remarkable example of how the EEE framework can be applied to personal growth.

In the execution phase, Rowling wrote the manuscript for Harry Potter and the Philosopher's Stone while struggling with financial hardship and personal challenges. However, despite the execution of her idea, she faced multiple rejections from publishers. Each rejection became an opportunity to evaluate her approach, from refining her manuscript to improving her pitch.

Rather than giving up, Rowling evolved. She persisted and finally secured a deal with Bloomsbury, a small publisher that saw potential in her work. Even after her book became successful, Rowling didn't stop evolving. She continued refining her storytelling with each subsequent book, creating an ever-expanding universe that captivated readers worldwide.

Rowling's personal story exemplifies the EEE framework as a tool not only for overcoming failure but for turning setbacks into stepping stones toward success. Her perseverance shows that execution must be paired with reflection and adaptation to reach greater heights.

Arnold Schwarzenegger: From Bodybuilder to Actor to Politician

Arnold Schwarzenegger's rise to fame and influence in various fields is another powerful story of the EEE process. Arnold began by executing his vision of becoming a world-class bodybuilder, winning Mr. Universe at the age of 20. However, he didn't stop at bodybuilding. He evaluated his success and recognized that he could leverage his fame to enter the entertainment industry.

After facing initial rejection in Hollywood due to his strong accent and muscular physique, Schwarzenegger evolved by improving his acting skills, working on his language, and choosing roles that suited his strengths. His breakthrough came with Conan the Barbarian and later The Terminator. Once again, he didn't rest on his laurels; he shifted his focus from entertainment to politics, eventually becoming the Governor of California.

Arnold's ability to continuously execute his plans, evaluate his position, and evolve in different fields is a testament to how the EEE framework can be applied to diverse life goals.

3. Scientific Breakthroughs: Innovating Through Iteration

Dr. M.S. Swaminathan: The Father of India's Green Revolution

Dr. M.S. Swaminathan, widely regarded as the architect of India's Green Revolution, exemplifies the Execute, Evaluate, and Evolve (EEE) framework in the field of agricultural science. His work not only transformed India's agricultural productivity but also secured food security for the nation.

Execution: In the 1960s, India was facing severe food shortages, and the country relied heavily on imports to feed its growing population. Dr. Swaminathan executed a plan to introduce high-yielding varieties (HYVs) of wheat and rice, adapted from Mexico and the Philippines, to Indian farmlands. He worked closely with other scientists, including Nobel laureate Dr. Norman Borlaug, to develop and promote the use of these varieties in India.

Evaluation: Dr. Swaminathan continuously evaluated the progress of the Green Revolution by assessing its impact on crop yields, farmers' livelihoods, and the environment. He noted that while the initial results were positive, there were concerns about the overuse of chemical fertilizers and water resources, as well as the environmental impact on soil fertility.

Evolution: To address these challenges, Dr. Swaminathan evolved his approach by advocating for sustainable agriculture practices. He emphasized the need for environmentally friendly technologies, crop diversification, and the inclusion of marginalized farmers in the benefits of the Green Revolution. His vision of "Evergreen Revolution" focuses on enhancing productivity without ecological harm. Dr. Swaminathan's ability to adapt the Green Revolution strategy to the changing agricultural landscape has left a lasting impact on India's food security and rural development.

This case shows how Dr. Swaminathan's application of the EEE framework helped India transition from a food-deficit nation to a self-sufficient agricultural powerhouse.

Dr. Vikram Sarabhai: The Visionary Behind India's Space Program

Dr. Vikram Sarabhai, the father of the Indian space program, is another notable Indian scientist who used the EEE model to lay the foundation for India's advancements in space technology.

Execution: Dr. Sarabhai, recognizing the potential of space technology for national development, founded the Indian National Committee for Space Research (INCOSPAR) in 1962, which later evolved into ISRO (Indian Space Research Organisation). His immediate focus was to execute the launch of India's first satellite and establish a robust space program. Under his leadership, the first experimental satellite, Aryabhata, was launched in 1975.

Evaluation: Sarabhai was constantly evaluating the global space race and India's position in it. He understood that India could not compete with superpowers like the US and the Soviet Union in military or large-scale space explorations, but he saw an opportunity to leverage space technology for socioeconomic development. He prioritized using satellites for communication, meteorology, and education, particularly in remote rural areas.

Evolution: Based on this evaluation, Sarabhai evolved India's space program to focus on practical applications. One of his key projects was the Satellite Instructional Television Experiment (SITE) in 1975, which used satellite technology to broadcast educational programs to over 2,400 villages across India. This groundbreaking project demonstrated how space technology could address issues like education, health, and communication in underserved regions. His strategic vision set the stage for India's later achievements in satellite technology and space exploration, including Chandrayaan and Mangalyaan missions.

Dr. Vikram Sarabhai's legacy shows how execution, continuous evaluation, and evolution can build a sustainable and impactful scientific program, positioning India as a significant player in global space research.

Thomas Edison: The Power of Persistence

Thomas Edison's journey in inventing the lightbulb is one of the most iconic stories of the EEE process in action. Edison was known for his relentless execution, conducting over 1,000 experiments in his quest to create a long-lasting electric lightbulb.

Each failed experiment became an opportunity for evaluation. Edison meticulously documented his results, constantly refining his designs based on what worked and what didn't. He famously said, "I have not failed. I've just found 10,000 ways that won't work," highlighting the value of persistent evaluation.

Edison's ability to evolve his experiments after each failure was crucial to his eventual success. His iterative approach to invention—trying, failing, learning, and adapting—allowed him to develop not just the lightbulb but numerous other innovations that have shaped the modern world, including the phonograph and motion picture camera.

Marie Curie: Evolving Through Scientific Discovery

Marie Curie, a pioneer in the field of radioactivity, exemplifies the EEE framework in scientific research. Her work, which led to the discovery of polonium and radium, required meticulous execution in a time when female scientists were largely marginalized.

Curie's dedication to evaluation was evident in her rigorous experimentation and her ability to challenge existing scientific theories. When her initial hypotheses faced scrutiny, Curie evolved her approach, expanding her research to isolate radioactive isotopes. Her ability to adapt her methods in the face of obstacles led to groundbreaking discoveries that earned her two Nobel Prizes.

Marie Curie's scientific breakthroughs demonstrate the value of using feedback loops and adaptation in the scientific process. Her legacy continues to inspire researchers to this day, proving that evolution in thought and practice is key to progress.

Conclusion: The Power of EEE in Every Field

Whether in business, personal growth, or scientific discovery, the EEE framework is a universal strategy for success. Above given examples show that executing a plan, evaluating the outcomes, and evolving based on feedback are crucial for innovation and growth. These stories highlight the transformative power of EEE and encourage readers to apply this framework in their own lives, no matter the field or challenge they face.

Chapter 6

TOOLS AND TECHNIQUES FOR EEE

The EEE (Execute, Evaluate & Evolve) framework, while conceptually simple, becomes highly effective when combined with the right tools and techniques. Whether for personal development, business, or innovation, using structured methods to track progress, reflect, and adapt is essential. This chapter explores practical tools and methodologies that empower individuals and organizations to execute plans, evaluate progress, and evolve toward greater success.

1. Journaling for Evaluation

Journaling is a simple yet powerful tool for self-reflection, evaluation, and growth. Psychological research has demonstrated the benefits of journaling in enhancing personal development, decision-making, and problem-solving abilities. By regularly writing down thoughts, experiences, and observations, individuals gain greater clarity on their progress and areas for improvement.

The Power of Reflection: Studies show that journaling helps the brain process events, emotions, and decisions, fostering self-awareness. According to a study published in the Journal of Experimental Psychology, those who journal daily showed higher levels of emotional regulation and problem-solving ability than those who didn't. This aligns with the EEE framework—journaling enables the evaluation phase by providing a concrete means of looking back at one's execution.

How to Use Journaling for EEE:

Daily Execution Logs: At the end of each day, write down what actions were taken and what outcomes were observed.

Weekly Evaluation: Every week, reflect on successes, challenges, and lessons learned. What strategies worked? What needs to be improved?

Monthly Evolution Checkpoints: Use monthly summaries to track how your approach has evolved. What habits, skills, or approaches have you adjusted to get closer to your goals?

Journaling, thus, serves as a mirror for self-evaluation and helps in evolving through continuous reflection.

2. Agile and Lean Methodologies

Originally designed for software development, Agile and Lean methodologies are models of EEE in action. Both emphasize flexibility, quick iteration, and constant feedback—making them applicable in diverse contexts such as business, project management, and even personal growth.

Agile: The Agile methodology focuses on iterative development, where small, manageable tasks are executed in short cycles (called sprints). Each sprint is followed by a retrospective evaluation to determine what went well and what can be improved in the next cycle. Agile's core principle is adaptability, ensuring that as goals evolve, so does the strategy.

Execution: Agile breaks down a large goal into smaller, achievable tasks. Teams or individuals execute these tasks in short periods, making it easier to track progress.

Evaluation: After each cycle, teams evaluate their work in a feedback session (retrospective). This aligns with the evaluate phase of EEE, where continuous feedback helps improve performance.

Evolution: Based on evaluation, adjustments are made for he next cycle, promoting constant evolution.
Lean: Lean methodology is rooted in eliminating waste and increasing efficiency. In business, this could mean cutting down on unnecessary steps, and in personal development, it can mean eliminating distractions or inefficiencies in time management. Lean's emphasis on continuous improvement mirrors the EEE model perfectly.

Execution: Focus on delivering value quickly and eliminating unnecessary steps.

Evaluation: Regularly assess what is adding value and what is waste.

Evolution: Continuously improve the process by making small, incremental changes.

Both Agile and Lean are highly adaptable to any context and help streamline execution while fostering constant improvement and evolution.

3. Growth Metrics

Measurable goals and key performance indicators (KPIs) are critical for the evaluate phase in the EEE framework. Without clear metrics, it's impossible to gauge success or identify areas that require adjustment.

Setting Measurable Goals: Goals should be SMART—Specific, Measurable, Achievable, Relevant, and Time-bound. By setting clear goals with measurable outcomes, you can track whether your execution is driving the desired results.

Specific: Define exactly what you aim to achieve (e.g., increase sales by 20%).

Measurable: Identify how you will measure success (e.g., tracking monthly sales growth).

Achievable: Ensure the goal is realistic given your resources and timeframe.

Relevant: Align your goals with larger strategic objectives (e.g., expanding market share).

Time-bound: Set a deadline for when you expect results (e.g., achieve the target within 6 months).

KPIs for Evaluation: KPIs are specific metrics used to measure progress and performance. For personal development, this could mean tracking habits, hours spent on learning, or milestones achieved. In business, KPIs can include customer satisfaction, revenue growth, or market penetration. KPIs are essential for the evaluation phase of EEE because they provide concrete data to assess whether current strategies are working.

Example KPIs for personal growth: Number of hours spent on skill development, number of new opportunities pursued, completion of tasks.

Example KPIs for business: Customer retention rate, net profit margins, return on investment (ROI).

Evolving Based on Metrics: Once KPIs are evaluated, the next step is to evolve. For instance, if a business's customer retention rate is lower than expected, it may need to evolve its customer service strategy. Similarly, if a personal growth metric like hours spent on learning isn't yielding results, you may need to evolve your learning strategy or choose more relevant materials.

4. Mind Mapping for Evolution

Mind mapping is a creative tool that helps visualize connections between ideas, making it easier to evolve new strategies based on past experiences and evaluations. By organizing your thoughts, actions, and results in a visual format, you can better understand patterns and identify areas for innovation.

How Mind Mapping Supports EEE

Execution: Start by mapping out all tasks and steps related to a particular project or goal.

Evaluation: Use the map to break down what worked and what didn't, identifying successes and obstacles.

Evolution: Map out potential solutions or new strategies based on the evaluation, allowing for creative brainstorming and innovation.

Mind maps provide a clear path for evolution by enabling you to visualize the connections between past performance and future strategy.

5. Feedback Loops

Feedback loops are essential for both personal and professional evolution. They ensure that execution is constantly being evaluated and refined based on real-world results. In the EEE framework, feedback loops serve as the continuous connection between evaluation and evolution.

Types of Feedback Loops:

Internal Feedback: Personal reflection, journaling, or team evaluations.

External Feedback: Client feedback, market response, mentor guidance, or peer reviews.

Using Feedback Loops: Regularly integrate feedback into your evaluation phase to ensure that your strategies remain relevant and effective. The quicker you incorporate feedback into your process, the faster you can evolve.

Conclusion

Tools like journaling, Agile and Lean methodologies, growth metrics, mind mapping, and feedback loops provide a structured way to implement the EEE (Execute, Evaluate & Evolve) framework in any area of life. By incorporating these techniques, individuals and organizations can refine their execution, gain valuable insights through evaluation, and continue evolving toward lasting success. These tools help create a cycle of continuous improvement, where each iteration builds on the last, driving exponential growth and progress.

Chapter 7

THE SCIENCE OF LONG-TERM SUCCESS

Long-term success is not a random achievement; it's the product of a deliberate process that integrates strategy, psychology, and consistent effort. In this chapter, we will delve into the scientific foundations behind sustained achievement, focusing on three critical pillars: the Progress Principle, Flow, and Positive Psychology. Each of these concepts reinforces the importance of the Execute, Evaluate, and Evolve (EEE) cycle, and how applying this formula over time can generate extraordinary results.

The Progress Principle: Small Wins, Big Gains

In her research on creativity and motivation, Teresa Amabile introduced the concept of the Progress Principle—the idea that even small wins can significantly boost engagement, motivation, and long-term progress. This principle emphasizes that success doesn't always come from major breakthroughs but rather from consistent, incremental steps forward.

When we execute a task, no matter how small, we create a sense of accomplishment. This feeling of progress fuels motivation, making it easier to evaluate and evolve our strategies moving forward. By repeatedly going through the Execute, Evaluate, and Evolve cycle, we harness the power of small wins, which build up over time, leading to substantial progress.

Amabile's research shows that the sense of progress is the most important driver of performance, even more so than external rewards. This idea perfectly aligns with the EEE framework. Each phase of executing, followed by evaluation and evolution, allows us to gain insights, adapt, and celebrate those micro-victories. The continuous loop of small achievements keeps us on track, building momentum toward larger goals.

Flow and Peak Performance

Renowned psychologist Mihaly Csikszentmihalyi's concept of Flow refers to a state of complete immersion in an activity where time seems to disappear, and we perform at our best. Achieving Flow is not just a matter of chance; it results from consistently executing challenging tasks that push our skills to the limit while keeping them within our capacity to succeed.

Flow often occurs when our abilities are stretched but not overwhelmed, creating a perfect balance between skill and challenge. The EEE cycle plays a crucial role in this. Through consistent Execution of tasks, followed by Evaluation of performance, we gradually evolve our skills and adapt our challenges, making it easier to enter and sustain Flow states.

Csikszentmihalyi explains that Flow is essential for peak performance—it enhances creativity, productivity, and satisfaction. When we're in Flow, we feel fully aligned with the task at hand, leading to more effective and efficient outcomes. The EEE cycle fosters this state by ensuring we continuously refine our approach to stay within the sweet spot of challenge and skill, where Flow thrives. Over time, this mastery leads to long-term success in both personal and professional domains.

Positive Psychology: Building Resilience and Growth

Martin Seligman, the father of Positive Psychology, highlights the importance of positive emotions, resilience, and personal strengths in achieving long-term success. His research shows that positive emotions not only enhance well-being but also broaden our thinking and improve our ability to problem-solve. This is especially relevant during the Evaluate and Evolve phases of the EEE cycle, where reflection and adaptation are key.

One of Seligman's most important contributions is the concept of resilience—the ability to bounce back from setbacks and continue progressing toward goals. In the pursuit of long-term success, setbacks are inevitable. However, the EEE cycle provides a structure to navigate challenges effectively. After every execution, we evaluate not just our successes but also our failures, enabling us to evolve and adapt. The process helps build resilience as we learn from mistakes and refine our strategies.

Seligman's theory also underscores the value of optimism and positive emotion in fostering creativity and innovation. When we approach challenges with a positive mindset, we are more likely to find solutions, persevere, and grow. This aligns perfectly with the EEE cycle's philosophy: evaluating with optimism and evolving with resilience sets the foundation for sustained success.

The EEE Cycle as the Engine of Long-Term Success
When combined, these three principles form the foundation of a science-backed approach to long-term success. The Progress Principle highlights the importance of small wins, Flow illustrates how consistent practice leads to peak performance, and Positive Psychology reminds us of the power of resilience and positive emotions. All three are inherently linked to the Execute, Evaluate, and Evolve process.

1. Execution: This phase taps into the Progress Principle by encouraging small wins and tangible progress, no matter how incremental. Execution puts theory into action, allowing you to build momentum.

2. Evaluation: Regular reflection on performance aligns with Positive Psychology's emphasis on resilience. Evaluating successes and failures from a place of optimism helps you learn from mistakes without losing sight of the bigger picture.

3. Evolution: The final stage is about adapting and growing based on insights gained during the evaluation phase. This phase allows for long-term Flow, as it keeps challenges at the right level for continuous growth. Evolution is where you fine-tune your approach and apply the lessons learned, making each iteration of the EEE cycle more powerful.

Conclusion: Mastering the Art of Progress

The science of long-term success is rooted in a continuous cycle of learning, adaptation, and improvement. Whether it's harnessing the motivational boost of small wins, finding Flow through optimal challenge, or building resilience through positive psychology, the EEE cycle encapsulates all the key elements necessary for sustained achievement.

By consistently executing, evaluating, and evolving, you not only move forward—you grow. This growth compounds over time, ensuring that long-term success is not just a possibility but a natural outcome of your daily efforts. The science is clear: follow the EEE track, and lasting success will follow.

Chapter 8

PRACTICAL APPLICATION OF EEE IN DAILY LIFE

The Triple EEE (Execute, Evaluate, Evolve) cycle isn't just a concept to be understood—it's a practical framework that can be applied across different areas of your life, from career progression to relationships and personal well-being. In this chapter, we'll explore how to bring the EEE cycle into your daily routine, demonstrating its power in transforming professional, personal, and health-related goals.

Applying EEE in Careers

Success in your career depends on consistent effort, strategic evaluation, and the willingness to adapt. Whether you're climbing the corporate ladder, transitioning careers, or seeking to improve your work performance, the EEE cycle can help you stay focused, assess progress, and pivot when necessary.

1. Execute: Start by setting clear career goals, both short-term and long-term. For example, if you're aiming for a promotion, your daily execution might involve improving a key skill, taking on leadership opportunities, or networking with colleagues. Break large goals into manageable tasks, and focus on executing these daily to build momentum.

2. Evaluate: After each project or major task, take time to reflect. How did you perform? What feedback did you receive? Use both quantitative (e.g., sales targets met, deadlines achieved) and qualitative measures (e.g., peer feedback, your sense of fulfillment). Regular self-assessment or reviews with mentors can highlight areas for growth.

3. Evolve: Based on your evaluations, be ready to evolve. This might mean learning new skills, seeking additional training, or changing your work habits. If a career shift is in your plans, evolving could also mean rethinking your path and considering new opportunities. The EEE cycle encourages continuous development, ensuring you never become stagnant in your career.

A real-world example comes from career transitions. Let's say someone in marketing wants to move into data analytics. The Execution phase would involve acquiring technical skills, such as mastering Excel or SQL. Evaluation might consist of seeking feedback from peers or tracking progress on projects. Evolving might then lead to a decision to specialize further or pursue certification courses. Over time, this person uses the EEE cycle to shift into a data-driven role with confidence.

Relationships and Social Life

The EEE cycle isn't just for career success; it can also transform personal relationships. From family dynamics to friendships and romantic partnerships, communication, feedback, and growth are essential for maintaining and improving these connections.

1. Execute: Start by consciously practicing healthy communication habits—listening, expressing empathy, and being present. Small actions, like regularly checking in with loved ones or setting aside time for meaningful conversations, can serve as daily execution steps. Just as in any other area, consistency matters.

2. Evaluate: Periodically, reflect on your relationships. Are you satisfied with the quality of your connections? Are there areas where communication breaks down or where you feel misunderstood? Seek feedback from others and be open to their perspective. This may not always be easy, but it's crucial for growth.

3. Evolve: Once you have feedback, apply it. If you've learned that you need to communicate more openly, make that a priority. If someone expresses the need for more time or attention, adjust your schedule to make room for them. Evolution in relationships is about making incremental adjustments that lead to deeper, more fulfilling connections.

For example, in a romantic relationship, executing might involve regular date nights or open communication about each other's needs. Evaluating could involve discussing how these actions have improved or strained the relationship, while evolving might mean setting new boundaries or revising routines to maintain harmony. By continually applying the EEE cycle, relationships can grow stronger and more resilient over time.

Health and Wellness

Achieving lasting health and wellness often requires behavior change, and the EEE cycle provides a powerful framework for making and sustaining these changes. Research from behavior change experts like B.J. Fogg and his Tiny Habits method shows that small, consistent actions are the key to building long-term habits, perfectly aligning with the EEE model.

1. Execute: The first step to improving your health is taking consistent action. Whether it's improving your diet, exercising regularly, or practicing mindfulness, execution means doing something every day that moves you closer to your wellness goals. Fogg's research shows that starting small—such as doing two push-ups a day or adding one vegetable to a meal—can create momentum. Execution should be manageable and sustainable.

2. Evaluate: After a few weeks of executing your plan, evaluate its effectiveness. Are you seeing the results you hoped for? How do you feel—physically, mentally, and emotionally? For example, if you've been following a new diet, assess whether you feel more energized or if you've met specific health targets like weight loss or improved lab results. Regularly check in with yourself or a coach to track progress.

3. Evolve: Based on your evaluation, make adjustments. If a specific diet isn't working, you might evolve your plan by trying a different eating pattern. If your exercise routine is too intense, you might scale it down to prevent burnout. Evolution ensures that your health strategy is flexible and adaptable, helping you overcome obstacles and stay committed to your goals.

For example, someone aiming to run a marathon might begin with executing a daily running habit. After a few weeks, evaluating their performance could reveal areas needing improvement, such as endurance or injury prevention. Evolving could mean incorporating cross-training or working with a coach to adjust their training plan. The EEE cycle ensures that progress in health and fitness is steady, sustainable, and responsive to personal needs.

Conclusion: EEE as a Daily Life Blueprint

The power of the EEE cycle lies in its versatility. Whether you're striving for professional success, stronger relationships, or better health, the cycle of executing, evaluating, and evolving can be applied to every area of your life. Its simplicity makes it accessible, while its emphasis on reflection and adaptation ensures continuous improvement.

By embedding the EEE framework into your daily life, you create a structure for achieving lasting success in any domain. The key is consistency—small, manageable steps that, when evaluated and evolved, lead to long-term growth and achievement. Whether it's in the workplace, your social circle, or your wellness journey, the EEE cycle will keep you moving forward, ready to adapt and excel no matter the challenge.

In the following chapters, we'll explore how to overcome common obstacles that arise during the EEE process, ensuring that you stay on track and continue evolving toward your long-term goals.

Chapter 9

CHALLENGES IN THE EEE PROCESS

The Triple EEE (Execute, Evaluate, Evolve) cycle is designed to drive continuous progress, but it's not always a smooth journey. Along the way, you'll encounter setbacks, discomfort from stepping outside your comfort zone, and the risk of stagnation after success. In this chapter, we'll address these common challenges and offer strategies grounded in psychological research to overcome them and stay on track toward lasting success.

Dealing with Setbacks

No journey toward success is free from setbacks. In fact, the evaluation phase of the EEE process often reveals areas where we've fallen short or outright failed. However, setbacks are not the end; they are a vital part of the growth process.

The Psychology of Resilience

Resilience is the ability to bounce back from failure and adversity, and it's critical in the EEE process. According to psychological research, setbacks trigger a variety of emotional responses—frustration, fear, and self-doubt. But these emotions can be managed with the right mindset. Psychologist Martin Seligman's work on learned optimism suggests that individuals who see setbacks as temporary, specific, and external (rather than permanent, pervasive, and personal) are more likely to persevere and adapt.

1. Execute: When setbacks occur, it's essential to maintain forward momentum, even if it's in small ways. The key is to keep executing and not let a failure halt progress entirely. It might mean adjusting your approach or breaking goals into even smaller steps that feel more achievable after a setback.

2. Evaluate: View setbacks as opportunities for learning rather than signs of defeat. Ask, "What went wrong?" and "What can I learn from this?" Developing a mindset that sees failure as feedback helps maintain focus on long-term goals, rather than getting stuck in the immediate disappointment of the failure.

3. Evolve: Once the lessons from failure are clear, the next step is to evolve. This is where resilience comes into play. Evolution means taking the lessons learned from setbacks and applying them in new ways—whether by changing your strategy, adopting a new habit, or seeking additional resources to prevent similar issues in the future.

Example: Consider an entrepreneur whose startup fails after two years. By applying the EEE cycle, they might begin by executing small steps like networking or refining a new business idea. Their evaluation would involve an honest look at why the first venture didn't succeed—perhaps market research was lacking, or the product didn't meet consumer needs. Evolution, in this case, might mean pivoting to a different market or learning new skills. Setbacks become stepping stones when approached with resilience and the EEE mindset.

Breaking Out of Comfort Zones

Evolution in the EEE cycle often demands leaving behind what is comfortable and familiar. This can be one of the biggest psychological hurdles in the process, as fear of failure and the unknown often hold people back from evolving.

The Psychology of Fear and Comfort Zones

Psychologist Carol Dweck's research on the fixed vs. growth mindset shows that individuals with a growth mindset embrace challenges and view discomfort as part of learning. In contrast, those with a fixed mindset avoid challenges to protect their sense of competency. In the EEE cycle, evolution requires stepping outside the comfort zone, pushing into areas that may cause anxiety or fear.

1. Execute: To evolve, you must first execute actions that push you out of your comfort zone. This could mean taking on a leadership role, pursuing a new career path, or developing a skill you've avoided. The discomfort experienced in these moments is a sign of growth, and regular practice makes it easier over time.

2. Evaluate: When stepping outside your comfort zone, it's important to regularly evaluate your progress, not just in terms of success, but in terms of personal growth. How have you expanded your skills, knowledge, or confidence? This reflective practice helps shift the focus from discomfort to growth.

3. Evolve: Evolution in this context means embracing the idea that discomfort is necessary for progress. Each time you face a fear or challenge, you're training your brain to be more adaptable. The more often you evolve through discomfort, the more resilient and capable you become.

Example: A professional who fears public speaking might begin by executing small steps, such as presenting to a small group. Over time, their evaluation might show increased confidence and skill, even if initial performances were shaky. As they continue to evolve, they may take on larger audiences or more complex speaking engagements, ultimately becoming a strong communicator. Breaking out of the comfort zone is essential for evolution.

Avoiding Stagnation

After experiencing success, there's a natural tendency to become complacent. However, long-term success requires continuous evolution. The risk of stagnation is particularly high when the initial goals of the EEE cycle have been met, and it feels easier to coast than to push forward.

The Human Need for Growth

Psychologists like Abraham Maslow and Mihaly Csikszentmihalyi emphasize the human need for growth and fulfillment. Maslow's hierarchy of needs places self-actualization—the continuous pursuit of personal growth—at the top. Similarly, Csikszentmihalyi's concept of flow shows that individuals find the greatest satisfaction and happiness when they are engaged in activities that challenge them just beyond their current abilities.

1. Execute: After achieving a goal, it's crucial to set new, more challenging goals to maintain momentum. This doesn't necessarily mean starting from scratch, but rather finding new dimensions of the original goal to pursue. The key is to keep executing with a mindset of continuous improvement.

2. Evaluate: Regular evaluation ensures that you don't become too comfortable with your success. Even when things are going well, ask yourself, "What can I do better?" and "How can I improve further?" This prevents complacency and fosters a culture of continuous learning.

3. Evolve: Evolution after success means expanding your horizons. It might mean learning new skills, taking on a mentorship role, or branching into new areas of expertise. Complacency is the enemy of evolution, so finding ways to stretch yourself ensures that you continue to grow.

Example: After running a successful business, a founder might execute by diversifying their products or entering a new market. Evaluating their strengths and the challenges ahead helps them refine their strategy. Evolving could mean adopting new technologies or pursuing international expansion. By using the EEE cycle, they avoid the trap of stagnation and continue their growth trajectory.

Conclusion: Overcoming Challenges in the EEE Cycle

The challenges in the EEE process—setbacks, fear of stepping out of your comfort zone, and the temptation of stagnation—are inevitable but manageable. The key is to approach each challenge as part of the process, not a barrier. Resilience helps you navigate failures, discomfort pushes you to evolve, and a commitment to growth prevents stagnation.

By integrating psychological insights and strategies into the EEE cycle, you can face these challenges head-on and continue progressing toward long-term success. The journey isn't always easy, but it is always rewarding for those who embrace the process fully.

In the next chapter, we'll explore real-world case studies of individuals and organizations that have successfully implemented the EEE cycle, demonstrating its power in achieving enduring success.

Chapter 10

CONCLUSION
EEE AS A LIFELONG PRACTICE

As we've journeyed through the Triple EEE Track—Execute, Evaluate, and Evolve—it's clear that this framework is not just a temporary tool for achieving isolated successes. Instead, it is a lifelong practice designed to foster continuous growth, adaptability, and lasting success in all areas of life.

Continuous Evolution: A Lifelong Journey

One of the key principles of the Triple EEE process is that evolution never ends. At each stage of your life, whether personally or professionally, new challenges and opportunities will emerge. To navigate these successfully, you must remain open to change and willing to evolve.

The beauty of the EEE framework is its flexibility. It applies as much to small, everyday decisions as it does to large, life-altering ones. By consistently executing, you maintain forward momentum. Through evaluation, you make course corrections and learn from experience. And through evolution, you adapt to changing circumstances and continue to grow. This cycle ensures that you never become stagnant or complacent, but instead remain engaged in the pursuit of improvement and excellence.

Why Continuous Evolution Matters

The world is constantly changing—industries transform, relationships shift, and even our understanding of ourselves evolves over time. To stay relevant, fulfilled, and successful, we must be able to adapt to these changes, and the EEE framework gives us a structured way to do so.

As author James Clear notes in Atomic Habits, "You do not rise to the level of your goals. You fall to the level of your systems." The EEE cycle is precisely the kind of system that supports continuous improvement, ensuring that even when the external environment shifts, your personal growth remains on track.

The Power of Small Steps and Incremental Growth

Throughout this book, we've discussed the importance of small actions leading to significant outcomes. Teresa Amabile's research on the progress principle reminds us that even small wins can lead to meaningful progress over time. The Triple EEE framework aligns with this idea by breaking down large, daunting tasks into manageable steps.

Every time you execute, no matter how small the action, you are contributing to a larger goal. Every time you evaluate, you fine-tune your process and gain clarity on your next move. And with each evolution, you push yourself further, moving beyond your current limits.

By practicing the EEE framework consistently, these small steps compound over time, leading to profound personal and professional growth.

Embracing Change and Uncertainty

Change is inevitable, and uncertainty is part of life. However, with the EEE framework, you have a reliable path to navigate through these uncertainties. Rather than fearing change, the EEE approach encourages you to embrace it as an opportunity for growth.

When you accept that evolution is part of the process, it becomes easier to approach new challenges with curiosity and resilience. You are not just reacting to external pressures; you are actively seeking ways to grow, improve, and evolve. This mindset not only makes you more adaptable but also helps you view obstacles as opportunities.

Final Thoughts: The Path to Lifelong Success

Success is not a destination; it's a journey of continuous learning, adapting, and growing. The Triple EEE framework is your compass on that journey. Whether you are navigating a career transition, improving your relationships, or striving for personal wellness, the EEE cycle provides a reliable structure for making progress and achieving success.

1. Execute: Keep taking action, no matter how small, toward your goals.

2. Evaluate: Reflect on your progress regularly, learn from your experiences, and adjust your approach.

3. Evolve: Embrace change, step out of your comfort zone, and continue pushing yourself to grow.

The EEE cycle is not just a method for achieving immediate goals but a lifestyle—one that keeps you moving forward, expanding your potential, and finding fulfillment in the pursuit of excellence.

As you continue to apply this framework in your life, remember that setbacks, discomfort, and uncertainty are all part of the process. They are signals that you are evolving, growing, and stepping into new opportunities. The Triple EEE Track isn't just a formula for success—it's a mindset for lifelong growth.

So, embrace the journey. Keep executing, evaluating, and evolving, and you will find that success, in all its forms, is always within reach.